first book of
trains

Isabel Thomas

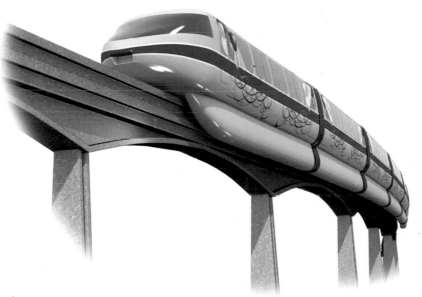

For Harry, Joey and Oscar

Published 2013 by
A&C Black
An imprint of Bloomsbury Publishing Plc
50 Bedford Square, London, WC1B 3DP

www.bloomsbury.com

ISBN 978-1-4081-9291-7

A CIP catalogue for this book is available from the British Library.

This book is produced using paper that is made from wood
grown in managed, sustainable forests. It is natural, renewable
and recyclable. The logging and manufacturing processes
conform to the environmental regulations of the country of origin.

Printed in China by C&C.

10 9 8 7 6 5 4 3 2 1

Contents

Train safety
Trains are powerful machines. They can be very dangerous.
Always have an adult with you when you look at trains.
Keep a safe distance away. Do not stand or play near railway
tracks, and never walk across railway tracks.

Trains

Railways run through towns and cities, across the countryside, and even underground. Look out for locomotives pulling wagons or carriages. Listen out for the whoosh of a steam engine or the blast of a train horn.

You can spot trains at stations, museums, and zooming past you on tracks. This book will help you to name the trains you see. It tells you how they work and shows you what special features to look out for.

At the back of this book is a Spotter's Guide to help you remember the trains you find. Tick them off as you spot them. You can also find out the meaning of some useful words here.

Turn the page to find out all about trains!

Steam locomotive

In the past, steam locomotives pulled most trains. You can still spot these old engines. Some are in museums. Others run on special railways.

Tank engines have a special store for water and coal. They do not have a tender.

Cab

Coal burned in firebox

Fuel and water are carried in the tender

These large wheels are turned by the engine

Steam locomotives burn coal. The fire heats water to make steam. The steam moves a piston back and forth. This turns the wheels.

Chimney

Boiler

Piston

Diesel-electric locomotive

A diesel-electric locomotive is pulling this train. The diesel engine powers a machine called a generator. This makes electricity. The electricity runs motors that turn the wheels.

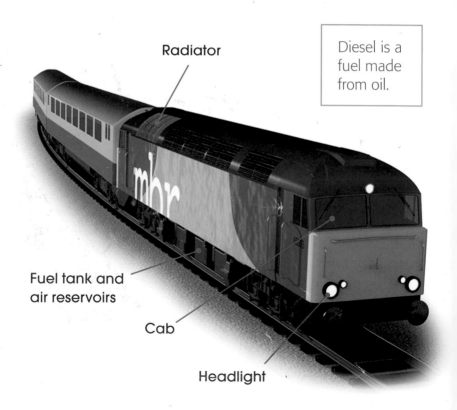

Radiator

Diesel is a fuel made from oil.

Fuel tank and air reservoirs

Cab

Headlight

Multiple unit train

This train does not need a locomotive. Each carriage can power itself. The driver controls them all from the front carriage.

Not every carriage in a multiple unit train needs to be powered.

There are diesel-powered and electric multiple unit trains.

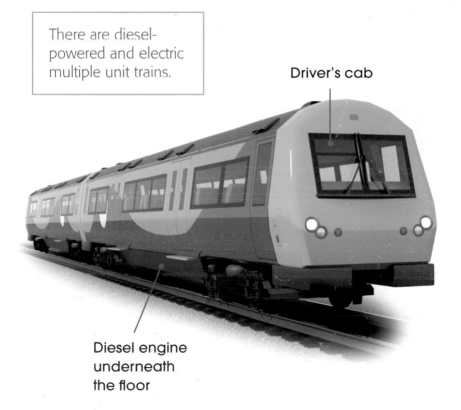

Driver's cab

Diesel engine underneath the floor

Electric locomotive

This locomotive is powered by electricity. It does not make any smoke. It is faster and quieter than a diesel-electric locomotive.

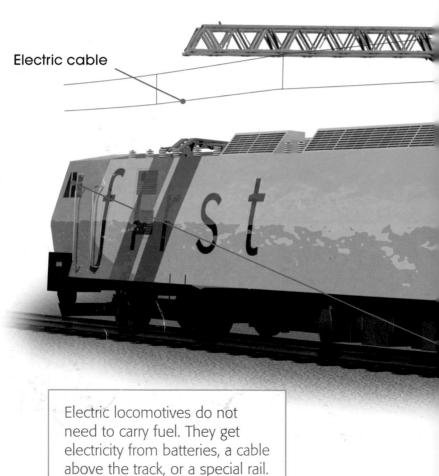

Electric cable

Electric locomotives do not need to carry fuel. They get electricity from batteries, a cable above the track, or a special rail.

Pantograph carries electricity from the cable to the train

Electric trains help to keep cities and towns free from pollution.

197265

Driver's cab at each end

Tram

Tram systems are a type of light railway. Trams travel on rails through city streets. They make frequent stops, like buses.

Most trams are electric, so there are no exhaust fumes.

Pole carries electricity to the tram

Electric cables

Screen shows destination

Station Street

Bendy joint between carriages

Low floor

Headlights

You might spot sand on tramway tracks. Sand helps the trams to brake.

Rails in the street

Cable car

This train does not need an engine or motor. A moving cable pulls it along. The cable is hidden underneath the track. The carriages grip the cable to move.

Cable cars always travel at the same speed. This is the speed that the cable moves.

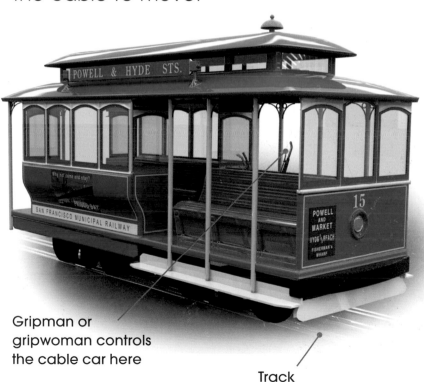

Gripman or gripwoman controls the cable car here

Track

Funicular

Funiculars are short, steep railways. They carry passengers up and down hills or mountains. Cables pull the cabins along the tracks.

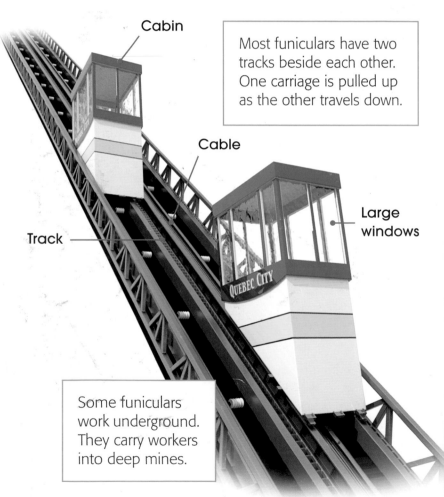

Cabin

Most funiculars have two tracks beside each other. One carriage is pulled up as the other travels down.

Cable

Large windows

Track

QUEBEC CITY

Some funiculars work underground. They carry workers into deep mines.

Driverless train

Not all trains need a driver. Computers drive this train. They can open and close the doors. They can even spot obstacles on the track.

Some driverless trains still have crew onboard to look after passengers.

Large window for passengers

Driverless trains are very safe. Computers don't get tired or make mistakes.

Passengers can sit right at the front of the train

Freight train

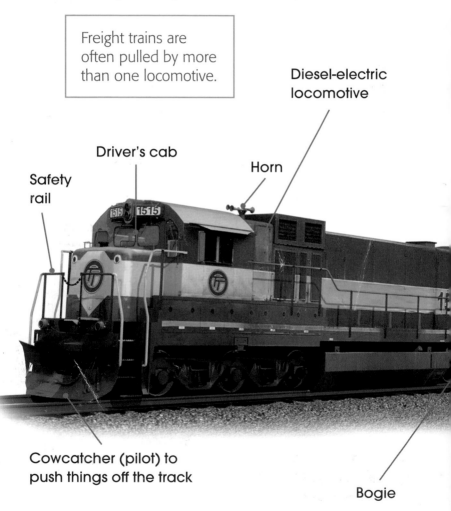

Freight trains carry goods instead of passengers. They are long and heavy. They travel slowly.

Freight trains are often pulled by more than one locomotive.

Diesel-electric locomotive

Driver's cab

Horn

Safety rail

Cowcatcher (pilot) to push things off the track

Bogie

Special wagons carry different types of goods, from cars to coal.

Some freight trains are more than a mile long!

Hopper wagon for loose material like stones

Tank wagon for liquids and gases

Flat wagon

Open wagon

TRANSOL

Low platform wagon

Some countries have special railways that only freight trains can use.

Local train

Local and regional trains stop at small stations as well as big stations. They carry passengers on short journeys. They travel at low speeds.

Regional trains are often multiple unit trains with no locomotive.

Lots of standing room for short journeys

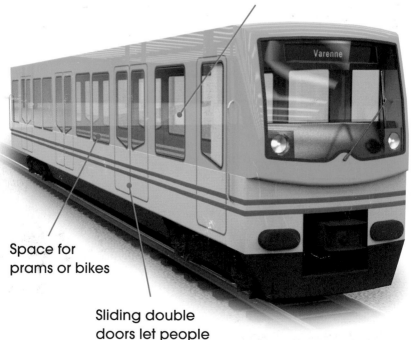

Space for prams or bikes

Sliding double doors let people on and off quickly

Intercity train

Intercity trains only stop at large stations in towns and cities. They have services on board to keep passengers comfortable on long journeys.

Many intercity trains have a shop on board, selling food, drinks, magazines and newspapers.

Tables for doing work, eating meals or playing games

Large, comfortable seats

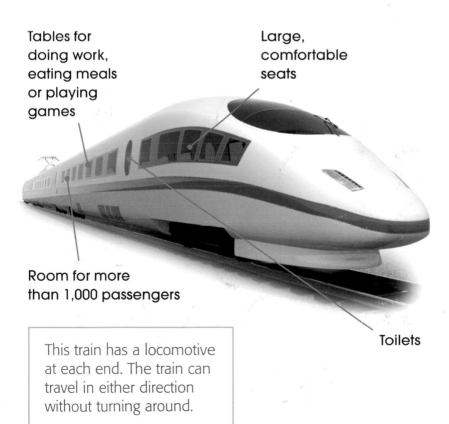

Room for more than 1,000 passengers

Toilets

This train has a locomotive at each end. The train can travel in either direction without turning around.

Multi-deck train

This carriage has seats on three levels. It can carry many more passengers than a normal carriage.

Trains can get very crowded as people travel to and from work. Multi-deck carriages provide extra seats without needing a longer train.

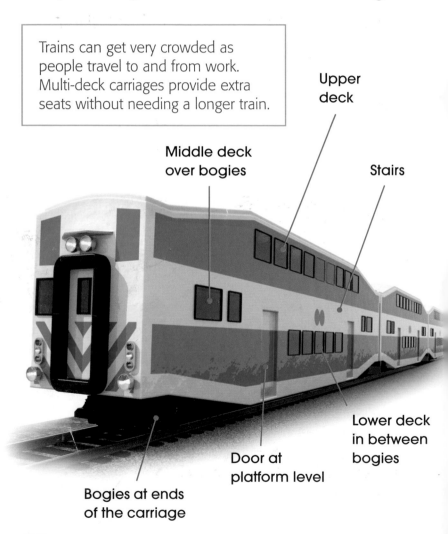

Upper deck

Middle deck over bogies

Stairs

Lower deck in between bogies

Door at platform level

Bogies at ends of the carriage

Car-carrying train

This motorail train has passenger carriages and car wagons. Passengers can take their car on the journey! People use trains like this to take their car or motorbike on holiday.

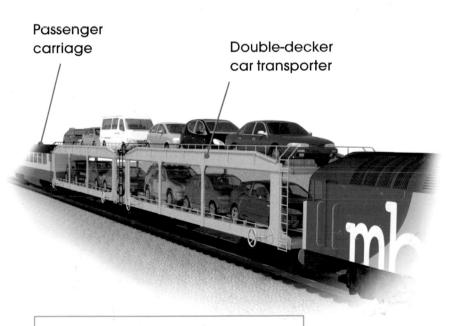

Passenger carriage

Double-decker car transporter

Eurotunnel is another type of car train. People drive their car on to the train. They stay in their car as they travel through the Channel Tunnel.

Tourist train

Many people take trains to
get to a holiday destination.
For other people, the train ride
is the holiday! Passengers take
this train to see the beautiful
countryside it travels through.

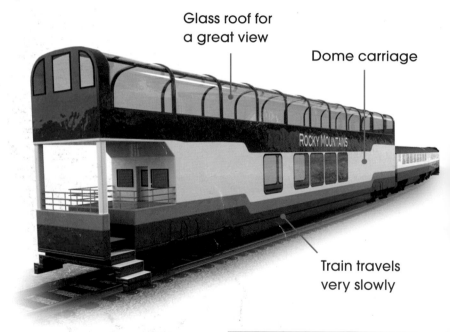

Glass roof for
a great view

Dome carriage

ROCKY MOUNTAINS

Train travels
very slowly

Passengers spend two
days onboard this Rocky
Mountaineer train.

Narrow gauge railway

The gauge of a railway track is the distance between the two rails. Narrow gauge railways have a small gap between the rails.

Trains on narrow gauge railways have to travel more slowly than trains on wider tracks.

Rails are less than 143.5 cm apart

High-speed train

High-speed trains are the fastest passenger trains. They often run on special tracks. Long, streamlined noses help them to travel quickly.

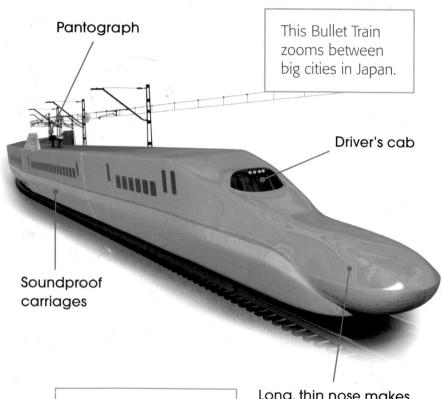

Pantograph

This Bullet Train zooms between big cities in Japan.

Driver's cab

Soundproof carriages

The fastest high-speed trains can travel up to 200 miles in one hour.

Long, thin nose makes the train less noisy as it zooms through tunnels

Container train

This freight train carries goods inside big metal boxes called containers. The containers are all the same size, but there may be different cargo inside each one.

Containers can be lifted off a train on to a ship, lorry, or aeroplane, without being unpacked.

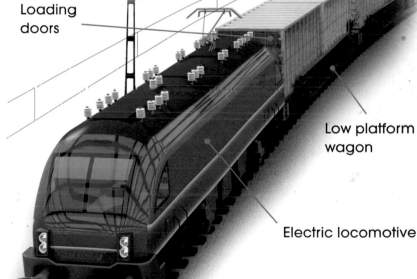

Metal container

Loading doors

Low platform wagon

Electric locomotive

Buffers

The containers sit on special low wagons.

 Maglev

This train has no wheels. Magnets make the carriages hover above the track! Magnets also make the train move. Maglev trains are super fast, smooth and quiet.

Maglev is short for magnetic levitation.

Train wraps around guideway

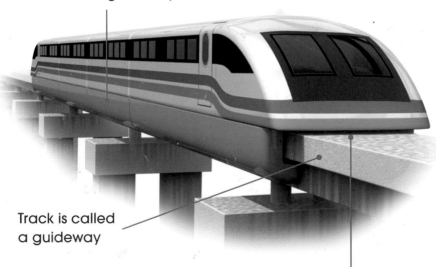

Track is called a guideway

Only a few countries have Maglev trains. This one is in Shanghai, China.

Train floats about 1 cm (a finger's width) above the track

Tilting train

A special trick helps this train to travel very fast. When it goes through a curve in the track, the train tilts. This keeps the ride smooth and comfortable.

Tilting trains are high-speed trains that do not need special tracks to travel fast.

Curved track

Train tilts in to the curve

Work train

Look out for huge work vehicles. They do different jobs on the railways. Some are machines for building or mending tracks. Others clean the tracks, and keep them free of weeds.

This machine helps to clean ballast (the crushed rocks that railway tracks sit on).

Work trains are often painted yellow

Elevated railway

You will need to look up to spot an elevated railway! They are built on high platforms. They can run through a city without getting in the way of people and cars.

Tracks above
street level

Singapore's elevated railway
saves space in the streets below.

Monorail train

Most railway tracks have two rails. But monorail trains run on just one rail. The trains are wider than the track. They wrap around the track so they can't fall off.

Most monorail trains are powered by electricity.

You might spot a monorail train at a theme park.

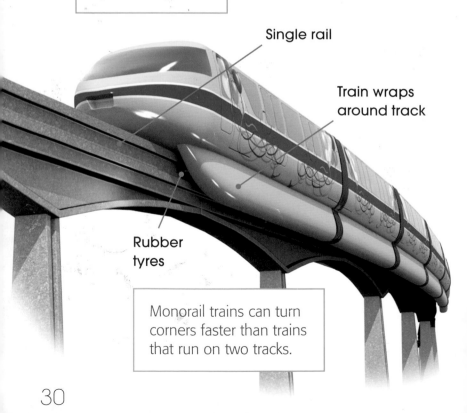

Single rail

Train wraps around track

Rubber tyres

Monorail trains can turn corners faster than trains that run on two tracks.

Suspended train

This train hangs underneath its track. Passengers have a great view. Travelling on board feels like floating through the air!

This train is suspended over a river in Germany.

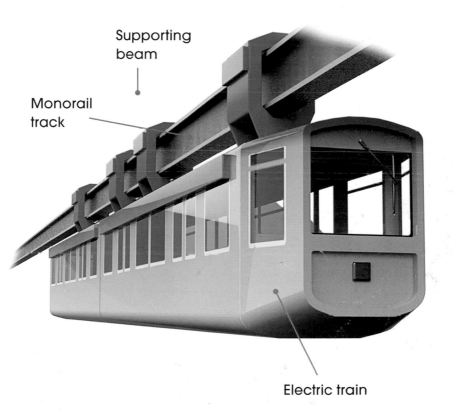

Supporting beam

Monorail track

Electric train

Underground train

Some big cities have underground railways. The trains travel through tunnels deep below the streets.

The world's oldest underground railway is in London, UK.

Wide aisles with space for lots of passengers to stand

Sliding doors to let people on and off quickly

Platform

Carriage floor at platform level

They carry people around quickly, without getting stuck in traffic jams.

Rounded roof to fit through tunnels

Headlight

Rubber-tyred underground train

Some underground trains have rubber tyres instead of steel wheels. They travel along special concrete tracks.

Main wheels with rubber tyres

Sideways wheels guide the train along the track

Back-up steel wheels and tracks

Cog railway

A normal train would slip down a steep track. This locomotive has an extra wheel with teeth, like a cog. The teeth fit into notches on a special middle rail.

Cog railways can climb mountains without slipping.

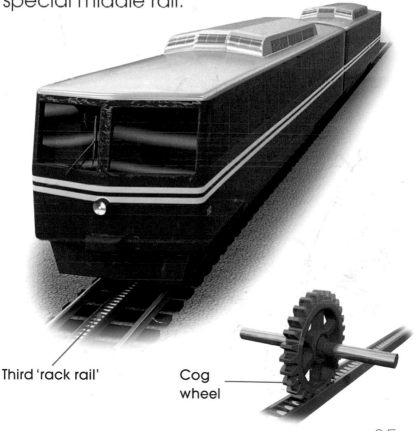

Third 'rack rail'

Cog wheel

35

Sleeper train

This famous train is a hotel on wheels. Passengers travel in private compartments with bathrooms. At night, the seats change into comfortable beds.

The Blue Train travels across South Africa.

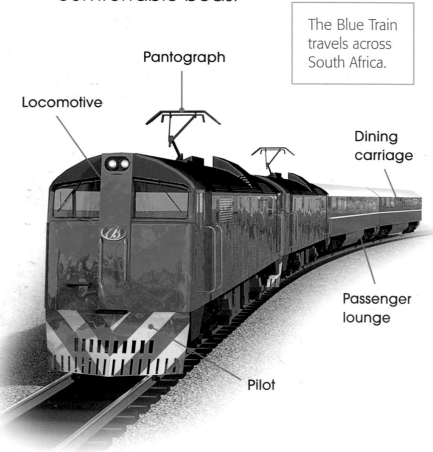

Pantograph

Locomotive

Dining carriage

Passenger lounge

Pilot

Royal train

A royal train is a special train used by a royal family. The British royal family uses this train. It has carriages for sleeping, dining, and working.

Special diesel locomotives are used to pull the Royal Train. They are painted dark red, like the carriages.

Carriages have grey roofs

Curtains

Royal Coat of Arms

Dark red paint

Rollercoaster

Rollercoasters are built for fun. Like other trains, they have carriages that are joined together and move along a track.

Wheels grip the track on three sides to stop the carriages falling off

Rollercoaster trains do not have engines. They are pulled up to the top of the first hill, or launched with a catapult.

But this track twists, turns, and may even loop the loop!

The trains roll around the rest of the track – like whooshing downhill on a bicycle!

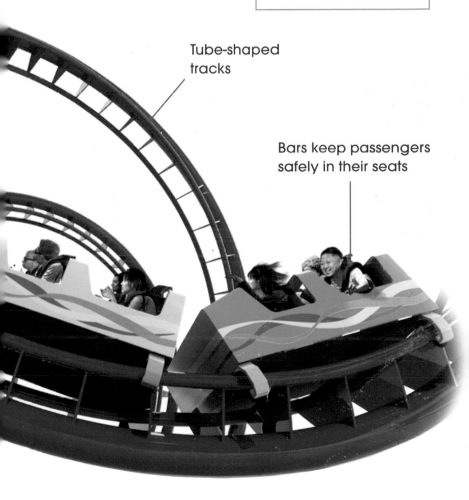

Tube-shaped tracks

Bars keep passengers safely in their seats

Personal rapid transit

These little pods are a mixture of train and taxi. The private carriages travel along a network of tracks. But they don't stop at every station. They only stop at the station you need!

You can spot personal rapid transit pods at Heathrow Airport in London, UK.

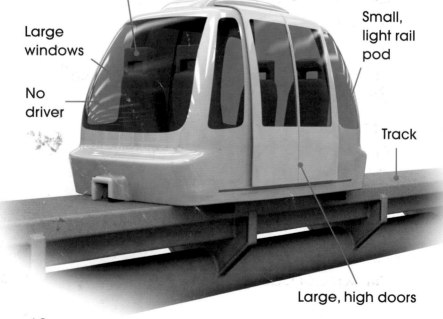

Seats for four people

Large windows

No driver

Small, light rail pod

Track

Large, high doors

Useful words

aisle the passage between rows of seats

bogie a frame with wheels, attached to the bottom of a locomotive or carriage

buffers pistons that absorb the shock when railway vehicles bump into each other

cab where the driver sits to control the train

carriage a passenger vehicle pulled by a locomotive

compartments areas inside a railway carriage that are separated by thin walls

light railway a railway that is smaller and less robust than a standard railway, used for less busy routes

locomotive a railway vehicle that has an engine or motor to make it go, and can pull a train

train a line of vehicles that are joined together, and travel along tracks

vestibule the space between two carriages or passenger compartments

Spotter's guide

How many of these trains
have you seen? Tick them
when you spot them.

 Steam
locomotive
page 6

 Diesel-electric
locomotive
page 8

 Multiple unit train
page 9

 Electric
locomotive
page 10

 Tram
page 12

 Cable car
page 13

 Funicular
page 14

 Driverless train
page 15

 Freight train
page 16

 Local train
page 18

 Intercity train
page 19

 Multi-deck train
page 20

 Car-carrying train
page 21

 Tourist train
page 22

 Narrow gauge railway
page 23

 High-speed train
page 24

 Container train
page 25

 Maglev
page 26

 Tilting train
page 27

 Work train
page 28

 Elevated railway
page 29

 Monorail train
page 30

 Suspended train
page 31

 Underground train
page 32

 Rubber-tyred underground train
page 34

 Cog railway
page 35

 Sleeper train
page 36

 Royal train
page 37

 Rollercoaster
page 38

 Personal rapid
transit
page 40

Find out more

If you would like to find out more about trains, you could visit a railway museum or heritage railway. These websites are a good place to start.

National Railway Museum York
www.nrm.org.uk

Heritage Railway Association
www.heritagerailways.com

London Transport Museum
www.ltmuseum.co.uk

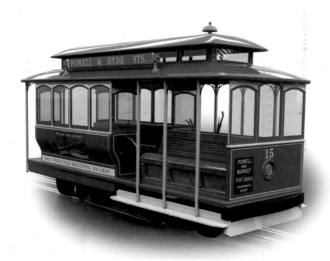